Celebrating Indigenous Peoples' Day

Katie Peters

GRL Consultant Diane Craig,
Certified Literacy Specialist

Lerner Publications ◆ Minneapolis

Note from a GRL Consultant
This Pull Ahead leveled book has been carefully designed for beginning readers. A team of guided reading literacy experts has reviewed and leveled the book to ensure readers pull ahead and experience success.

Lerner Publications
An imprint of Lerner Publishing Group, Inc.
241 First Avenue North
Minneapolis, MN 55401 USA

For reading levels and more information, look up this title at www.lernerbooks.com.

Main body text set in Memphis Pro 24/39
Typeface provided by Linotype.

Photo Acknowledgments
The images in this book are used with the permission of: © Nataliia K/Shutterstock Images, p. 3; © joi54/Shutterstock Images, pp. 4–5; © AnjelikaGr/Shutterstock Images, pp. 6–7, 16 (middle); © Bill Perry/Shutterstock Images, pp. 8–9, 16 (right); © Warren Price Photography/Shutterstock Images, pp. 10–11, 16 (left); © Nytia HENRIOT/Shutterstock Images, pp. 12–13; © SALMONNEGRO-STOCK/Shutterstock Images, pp. 14–15.

Front Cover: © Alina Reynbakh/Shutterstock Images

Library of Congress Cataloging-in-Publication Data

Names: Peters, Katie, author.
Title: Celebrating Indigenous Peoples' Day / Katie Peters.
Description: Minneapolis, MN : Lerner Publications, [2026] | Series: Let's celebrate holidays (Pull Ahead Readers – nonfiction) | Includes index. | Audience: Ages 4–7 | Audience: Grades K–1 | Summary: "Indigenous Peoples' Day helps us honor those who were here first. With easy-to-read text and vibrant photos, readers can learn how to celebrate native culture. Pairs with the fiction title, Winnie's Indigenous Peoples' Day"—Provided by publisher.
Identifiers: LCCN 2024038506 (print) | LCCN 2024038507 (ebook) | ISBN 9798765668733 (library binding) | ISBN 9798765684405 (paperback) | ISBN 9798765678657 (epub)
Subjects: LCSH: Indigenous Peoples' Day—Juvenile literature. | Indians of North America—Juvenile literature. | Holidays—United States—Juvenile literature.
Classification: LCC GT4995.I53 P42 2026 (print) | LCC GT4995.I53 (ebook) | DDC 394.264—dc23/eng/20240826

LC record available at https://lccn.loc.gov/2024038506
LC ebook record available at https://lccn.loc.gov/2024038507

Manufactured in the United States of America
1 – CG – 7/15/25

Table of Contents

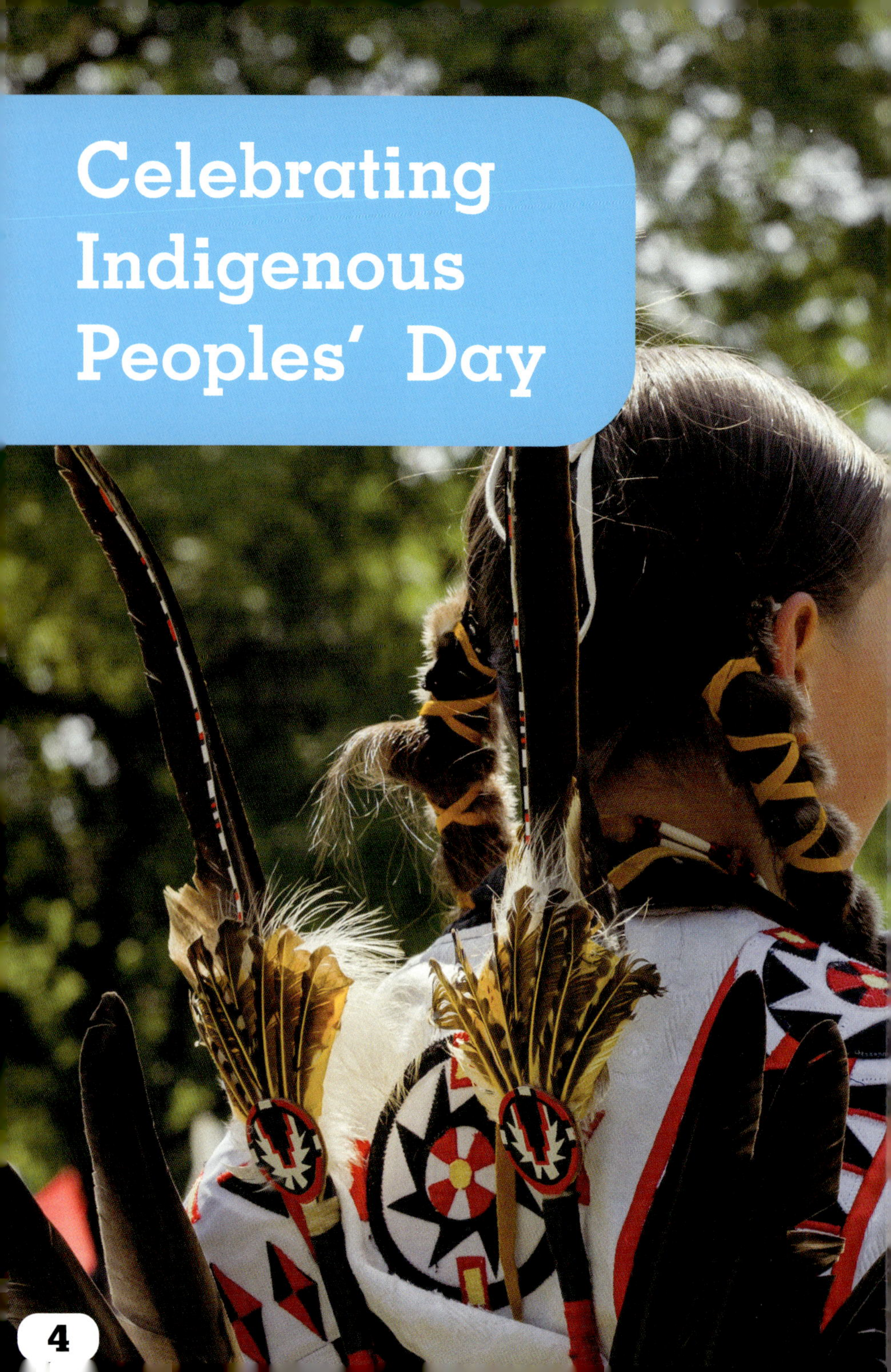

Celebrating Indigenous Peoples' Day

We were the first to live here.

We have our own food.

We make music.
We have our own music.

We make art. We have our own art.

We have our own flags.

We have the same rights as all people.

Did You See It?

art

food

music

Index